RACHEL MCLEAN'S DORSET CRIME TRAIL

Rachel McLean writes thrillers that make your pulse race and your brain tick. Originally a self-publishing sensation, she has sold millions of copies digitally, with massive success in the UK, and a growing reach internationally. She is the author of the Dorset Crime novels and the spin-off McBride & Tanner series and Cumbria Crime series. In 2021, she won the Kindle Storyteller Award with *The Corfe Castle Murders* and her last five books have all hit No1 in the Bookstat ebook chart on launch.

ALSO BY RACHEL MCLEAN

Dorset Crime series

The Corfe Castle Murders
The Clifftop Murders
The Island Murders
The Monument Murders
The Millionaire Murders
The Fossil Beach Murders
The Blue Pool Murders
The Lighthouse Murders
The Ghost Village Murders
The Poole Harbour Murders
...and more to come

RACHEL McLEAN's
Dorset Crime Trail

A walk through the dramatic Jurassic Coast locations
from the bestselling Dorset Crime series

Copyright © 2024 by Rachel McLean

All rights reserved.

No part of this book may be reproduced in any form or by any electronic or mechanical means, including information storage and retrieval systems, without written permission from the author, except for the use of brief quotations in a book review.

Ackroyd Publishing

ackroydpublishing.com

Printed and bound in the UK by CPI Group (Uk) Ltd, Croydon CR0 4YY

In memory of my mum Carol, who ignited my love for Dorset and continues to inspire me.

CONTENTS

Introduction	1
1. Corfe Castle and the Purbeck Way	5
2. Old Harry Rocks and Ballard Down	14
3. Brownsea Island	22
4. Durlston Head and Swanage	30
5. Sandbanks	40
6. Lyme Regis	48
7. Blue Pool and Wareham	56
8. Portland Bill	65
9. Tyneham and Worbarrow Bay	78
The Future...	87
Read the Dorset Crime Series	91
Also by Rachel McLean	93
Acknowledgements	95
Picture Credits	99

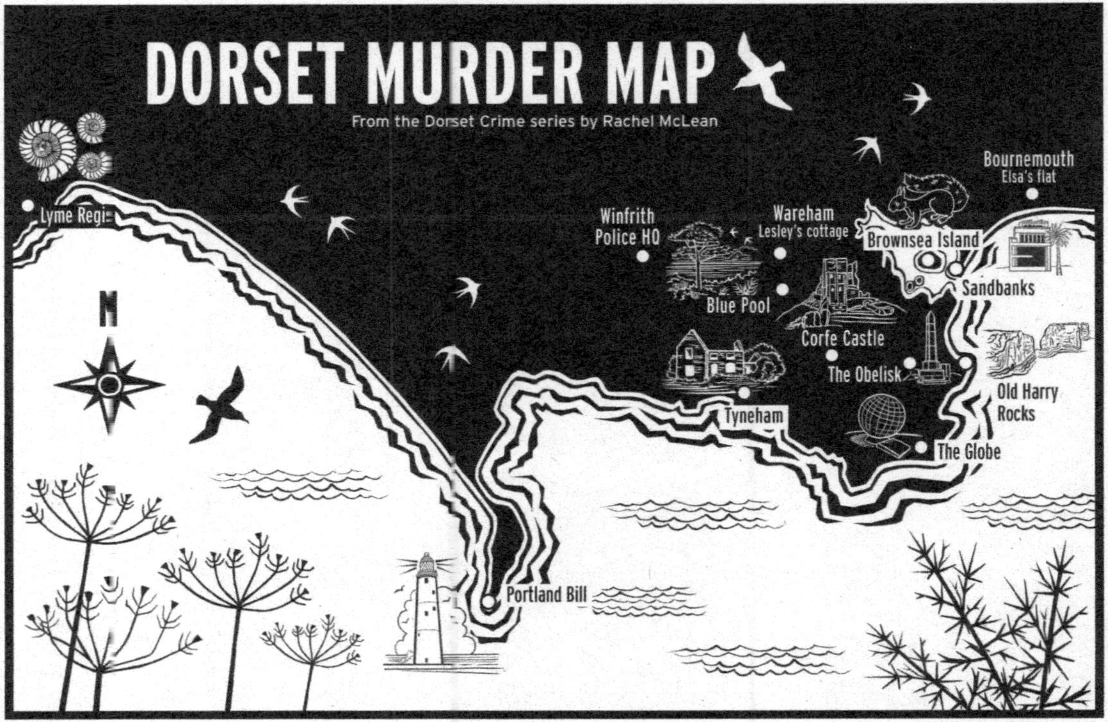

Illustration by Ma[illegible]a Burns

rachelmclean.com

INTRODUCTION
DORSET – THE PERFECT PLACE TO WRITE

I love Dorset.

The first time I visited the county was as a baby, taken to a hotel in Sandbanks (not *quite* as fancy in the 1970s) by my parents.

When I grew up, they enjoyed embarrassing me with the story of how difficult I was in the hotel room. The only way they could get me to sleep, or even to stop screaming for a moment, was to keep all the lights on. Unfortunately, *they* couldn't sleep unless the lights were off. The solution, in the end, was for them to haul the full-size hotel-issue cot into the bathroom, leave the light on, and shut the door. Bliss.

From the age of four I was visiting Swanage on a regular basis. My grandparents, parents, aunts, uncles and cousins would all descend on The Pines Hotel at the top of the cliffs. In those days, seaside hotels were quite formal places. I have distant memories of enjoying a special 'tea' in the restaurant, hours before all the adults took their dinner in the same space – heaven forbid that we children should be allowed to join in with that. Back then, the hotel was renowned for its cuisine, and on one occasion, my aunt trekked up the hill from the beach at lunchtime because she couldn't bear the thought of missing out on lunch at The Pines.

When I was a few years older, my parents decided to make their relationship with Dorset more formal. They bought a static caravan just outside Wareham, overlooking the River Frome. This being the late seventies, caravans didn't have mains electricity, and when we arrived (often late on a Friday, heading down from Birmingham as soon as my dad finished work) we would have to light the gas lights on the walls. They were incredibly fragile and I was terrified of breaking them – but not, bizarrely, of setting fire to myself in the process.

We kept that caravan for many years (and many years later, when I'd grown up, my parents bought another one in the exact same pitch). I adored it. The caravan site was full of children my age, and I would leave the van in the mornings and not see Mum and Dad again until evening. We would wade in the river, climb cliffs, stalk each other through fields of tall grass and befriend random dogs. The only things missing from the complete Enid Blyton experience were smugglers and lashings of ginger beer. Many of my formative memories are from Dorset: learning to swim at Swanage beach, learning to ride a bike in the country lanes around Wareham. It was wonderful.

So why am I telling you all this about my Dorset childhood? Well, it goes a long way to explaining why I chose to write crime novels set in the county, despite being a born and bred Brummie.

My first crime series – The DI Zoe Finch 'Deadly' books – was set in my home city of Birmingham. Those books were bestsellers and enabled me to become a full-time author. But when the series drew to a close and I started casting around for a location for my next series, Dorset was the obvious choice.

Moving one of my characters (the redoubtable DCI Lesley Clarke) to a new location with a new team, and expecting my readers to come along with me, felt like quite a risk. I was worried that the police procedural genre wouldn't fit quite so well in a rural location – these aren't cosy mysteries, after all.

I couldn't have been more wrong. At the time of writing, there are nine Dorset Crime books, and they've sold over a million copies and become the mainstay of my writing career. When I attend author events in Dorset, I'm always delighted to meet people who think of my characters as friends. I even watched while two readers had an argument over whether or not Lesley is a nice person. (Spoiler: she's not real!)

And the other (huge) benefit to writing about Dorset is that I get to spend time in the county on a regular basis, and pretend it's work. It's really not: it's fun. Every time I start work on a novel, I take the opportunity to walk around my locations. I find the spot where Lesley and her sidekick DS Dennis Frampton would park their cars, and I do the same walk to the crime scene they would do. Is it hilly? Muddy? Are there beautiful views (there always are)? And most importantly, which beauty spot can I ruin by (metaphorically) dumping a body in it?

Dorset continues to inspire me. I don't believe I'll ever run out of places to write about, and grisly ways for people to meet their end in those places. And there isn't enough time in the world to write all the locations I could feature. So if you've asked me to write about your village and I haven't yet got round to it, I'm sorry. There are just so many!

In this book, I'm going to share the county I love with you. Each chapter will focus on the locations in one of the books in my Dorset Crime series. I'll explain why I chose to write about that spot, give an overview (with no spoilers) of what happens there, and take you on a walk through the locations. I hope that by the time you've finished, you'll be inspired to get out into the Dorset countryside and walk through my locations, too. You won't regret it.

Happy reading!

1

CORFE CASTLE AND THE PURBECK WAY

ARCHAEOLOGY AND TEA SHOPS

Detective Chief Inspector Lesley Clarke sat at the wrought iron table, sizing up the cream tea in front of her. She looked across the idyllic garden towards one of the most iconic views England had to offer.

She drew a deep breath, forced herself to sit

upright, and wondered what the hell she'd done to deserve this.

She picked up her knife. Might as well make the best of it.

Jam first, or cream? She had a feeling the elderly couple who kept peering at her from the next table along would tut audibly if she got it wrong.

The Corfe Castle Murders, Chapter 1

My first Dorset Crime book, *The Corfe Castle Murders*, opens with a scene in the National Trust tearoom in the shadow of Corfe Castle. DCI Lesley Clarke is with her daughter Sharon, trying to order a beer. The ensuing confusion and frustration is directly lifted from the experience of a friend in that very tearoom some years ago – but I know from experience that the staff there are much friendlier now.

There couldn't be a much more iconic sight than the ruins of Corfe Castle pictured from the tables of a tearoom, and I took full advantage of the opportunity, snapping a photo of my cream tea with the castle in the background in the summer of 2021.

There was a problem, though. The world was just starting to open up again after the Covid-19 lockdowns, and my scones, jam and cream were served on a paper plate with a plastic cup of tea. Not quite the image I was after! At least I managed to get an angle blocking out the modern world.

Lesley doesn't stay in the tearoom for long – she hears a scream and is plunged into her first case the day before she officially begins her new job in Dorset's Major Crimes Investigation Team. And if you want to know what happens next, you'll need to read the book.

Why did I choose to kick everything off in Corfe Castle? Well, I'd already decided on Dorset for the series, and the Isle of Purbeck (which Corfe Castle sits at the heart of) was the area I knew best. The mental leap from

Purbeck to Corfe wasn't hard – it's one of England's most celebrated sights, after all.

I've been visiting Corfe Castle since I was a small child. In the seventies and eighties, you could climb all over the ruins, and I have old photographs of me and my cousins shouting at each other from the top of one wall to another. I also have photographs of my son rolling down the hill leading up to the castle, many years later. He was two at the time, and the rules had changed, but there's no way I would have let him climb even if he'd been allowed. Funny how your perception of danger changes when you're a parent.

But I have to admit, I hadn't paid much attention to the history of the castle – too busy clambering. So when I started researching the castle and the village for *The Corfe Castle Murders*, I was surprised.

As a child, I'd always assumed that the castle had naturally fallen into disrepair as a result of its age (please don't laugh). As an adult, I learned that the bulk of the damage was caused in a series of Civil War sieges, culminating in 1646. The Bankes family (whose influence can be seen all over Purbeck) were royalists, while the villagers were republicans. Corfe Castle was the last royalist stronghold in the area, and Lord Bankes was away fighting with King Charles, leaving Lady Bankes in charge. The perfect opportunity to take the castle, yes?

Well, not quite. Lady Bankes proved tougher than the locals expected, and led a defence effort that lasted several months. The Parliamentarian army bombarded the castle and made multiple attempts to breach the walls. But Lady Mary held strong.

It wasn't enough. Eventually her forces were overcome, and she fled to Kingston Lacy near Wimborne, avoiding injury or capture. Centuries later her descendants still owned the castle (along with Kingston Lacy), and gifted both to the National Trust in 1982, along with a large amount of land around Purbeck.

This explains why, if you're visiting Purbeck and planning to head to the beaches, it makes sense to join the National Trust so you can park for free in their car parks – there are a lot of those (as well as beaches) on former Bankes land.

Another thing I'd never really noticed as a child is the fact that the village is built from local Purbeck stone, the same stone as the castle. Did the villagers quarry that stone to build their homes and businesses?

To some extent, yes. But not entirely. A lot of that stone was simply stolen from the castle. After the siege, the castle was deliberately destroyed to prevent it being used as a royalist fortress again. The villagers proceeded to pilfer stone from its walls, and from the ruins created by the siege. But from all that destruction came something utterly beautiful: a castle and a village that complement each other perfectly.

If the aim had been to build a future tourist attraction, they really couldn't have done much better.

If you want to see how the village and castle complement each other, take a look at the model village on West

Street (almost everything in Corfe is on West Street, including the car park Lesley gets fed up of walking back and forth from). It's one of those perfect English tourist attractions that isn't the slightest bit glitzy, and has barely changed in decades. Just how a model village should be. And if you're into really tiny tourist attractions, try the Corfe Castle Museum – so small that only a few people at a time can get inside.

One of the reasons Corfe was a lone stronghold in the region for so long was its all-but-impregnable position. It's on a mound in the middle of the Purbeck Way, with magnificent views into the distance. From the ramparts of Corfe Castle you would have been able to see the full Purbeck coastline to the south and Poole Harbour to the north. Those views are still there, and relatively unspoilt, today.

My favourite spot to take in the view is at the top of Rollington Hill, the hill just to the west of Corfe Castle on the walk to Swanage. It's a steep climb, and it's tempting to give up, especially when for much of the way up all you can see at the top is a TV mast. But persevere – the view from the hill beneath that mast is stunning.

And it's a view I once had the opportunity to admire for quite a stretch of time.

When researching *The Corfe Castle Murders*, I walked from Corfe Castle to Swanage along the Purbeck Way, taking a leisurely day over it and working in many of the locations from *The Monument Murders* and *The Ballard*

Down Murder on the way. Only half an hour into my walk, I hit a problem, in the form of a herd of cows.

Yes, the landscape is vast and open up there. But there were a lot of cows, they were very big cows, and they were standing right where I wanted to go.

I could try and scare them off, or I could go back. I chose a third option – I took a little walk along a side path, sat down to eat my packed lunch and admire the view, and waited. By the time I'd finished, they'd moved along and it was safe to proceed. And I'd enjoyed my sandwiches in a glorious location (and found the perfect spot for the second crime scene in the book). Thanks, cows.

If you do make the walk, don't forget to turn around when you get to the top of the hill. The view back to Corfe Castle is dramatic, and if you're lucky you'll see the steam from one of the Swanage Steam Railway's trains as it plies its way to Swanage.

Yes, Corfe Castle sometimes feels like it's frozen in time, and living there might be challenging, as Lesley and the suspects in *The Corfe Castle Murders* discover. But it's an unmissable stop on any tour of Dorset, and the perfect place to locate a book.

Key book locations in Corfe Castle and around

- Corfe Castle
- West Street car park(!)
- The Pink Goat Café
- The Greyhound Inn
- Rollington Hill
- The Rings (a historical site just south of the castle)

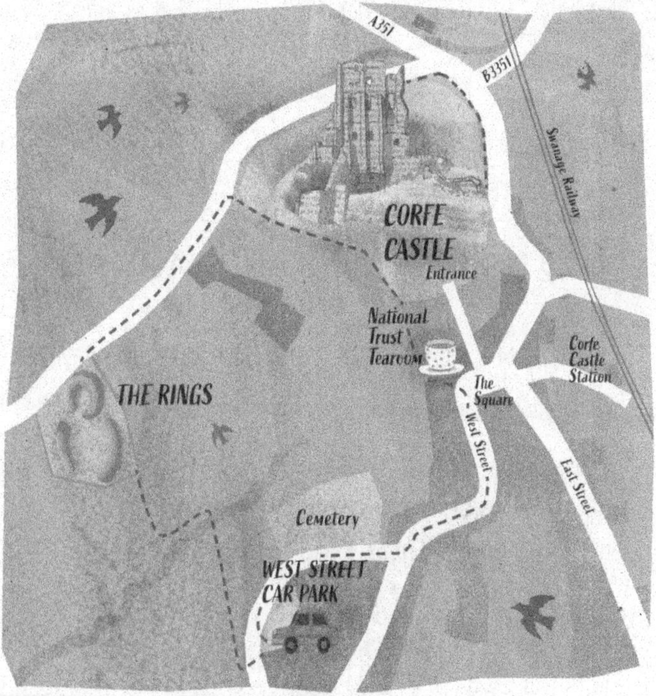

CORFE CASTLE AND THE PURBECK WAY

Corfe Castle

Walking route

West Street car park, Corfe Castle – The Rings – Corfe Castle (road along the northern edge) – Corfe Castle village – Corfe Castle entrance

2

OLD HARRY ROCKS AND BALLARD DOWN

WALKING TOWARDS THE ISLE OF WIGHT

Over to the east, the cliffs of The Needles were coming into view, sunrise approaching. It was brighter over there, not blurred by fog. With luck, there would be a perfect backdrop to her photo of Old Harry Rocks. Ameena wasn't a professional

photographer, but it had been a hobby for fifteen years.

The Clifftop Murders, Chapter 1

In the previous chapter, I introduced you to the walk from Corfe Castle up to the top of Rollington Hill, and the fabulous views you'll get from the top. (I didn't mention that in *The Corfe Castle Murders* I ruin that view with a dead body, forensic tents and a whole team of investigators. Sorry!)

If you've decided to take that walk, I strongly recommend continuing along the Purbeck Way towards Swanage. If you think you've already seen the best of the views, you're very much mistaken.

The Purbeck Way is a fifteen-mile walk from Wareham to Studland, which joins the Purbeck Ridge at Corfe. And the Purbeck Ridge is a line of limestone-topped hills, also stretching fifteen miles, from Worbarrow Bay in the west (which we'll encounter later in this book) to Swanage in the east.

As you walk towards Swanage, it becomes apparent that the limestone continues as far as the Isle of Wight. If you could keep walking, maybe jumping (or being pushed, if you have the misfortune to be a character in one of my books) from the clifftop at Old Harry Rocks, donning diving gear to stroll along the seabed, and emerging twenty miles further along that strip of limestone, you'd find yourself at The Needles, the Isle of Wight's closest point to Dorset.

The walk towards Old Harry Rocks is a beautiful one. It's a gentle uphill walk, the ground rising as you approach the sea, and if you can't face those few extra miles, there are plenty of points where you can peel off and head towards Swanage. And despite the number of people who walk that route, there's plenty of space and plenty of wildlife. When I walked the path in May 2021 (after my lunch hiding from the cows, as I mentioned in the previous chapter), I sat down to take in the surroundings and spotted a skylark racing into the sky just a few metres away. And in spring when you walk across Ballard Down, you can hear them all around you, nesting in the scrubby grass. (Tip: keep your dog on a lead!)

On a clear day, The Needles are easily visible from Purbeck. I have childhood memories of looking across the sea at them from the beach at Swanage. If you get the right angle, you can even get a photo of them in the distance, with Old Harry Rocks in the foreground. Sadly, the rocks are eroding fast and there aren't as many of them as there were when I was a child. The main pillar is Old Harry, then there's Old Harry's Wife, sadly without a name of her own, a little further out to sea, and other smaller stacks that are constantly eroding and changing shape.

The view of the rocks, and my attempts to capture it on camera during an excursion to Studland thirteen years ago, inspired the opening scene of *The Clifftop Murders*.

My children were very young, and I'd decided I needed a weekend to myself in the countryside. So I made for the Isle of Purbeck. Foolishly, I'd chosen to camp – and to carry my tent on my back. The less said about that, the better!

On the second day, I was determined to get a photo of Old Harry Rocks. So I left Swanage on the bus, where I was staying at the youth hostel (it was pouring with rain, and I'd given up on the tiny, leaky tent) and headed up the coast. The rain was easing off, and I thought I'd get lucky.

No such luck. As I climbed down from the bus, the heavens opened. The trickle of people heading along the path from the clifftop to the road became a stream – everyone else was doing the sensible thing, and leaving.

But my next bus wasn't for an hour. And as I approached the clifftops, I spotted the sun shining over Bournemouth in the distance.

If the sun was shining there, then surely the gap in the clouds would move south, and soon be over my head. And *that* would mean a rainbow.

So I sat down. I picked the driest spot I could find, spread my coat around me (without taking it off, I wasn't that daft), and waited. For an hour.

Finally the rainbow arrived, and I got my photographs. By the time I had finished, the sun was shining and I decided to take the coastal path back into Swanage.

I love that stretch of the coastal path. The first time I took it, I was small enough to be riding on my dad's shoulders, with various family members walking alongside us – my uncle and cousins, if I remember rightly. It's a relatively easy walk from Swanage to Studland, and there are good pubs at both ends of the path and a bus route linking the two. What's not to like?

So when I was looking for a location for the second book in the series, *The Clifftop Murders*, Ballard Down, Old Harry Rocks and my day waiting for a rainbow came to mind. Ameena Khan, who sadly comes to a sticky end right at the beginning of the book, is a keen amateur photographer, like me. But instead of waiting for a rainbow, she's waiting for the dawn. The cliffs in that spot face almost due east, so she'll get a stunning shot of the sun rising over the sea.

Or she would have done, if somebody hadn't pushed her off the cliff...

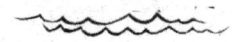

Key book locations at Ballard Down and around

- Ballard Down
- Old Harry Rocks
- Studland
- The Obelisk (see Chapter 4)
- Swanage and Ulwell

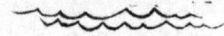

OLD HARRY ROCKS AND BALLARD DOWN

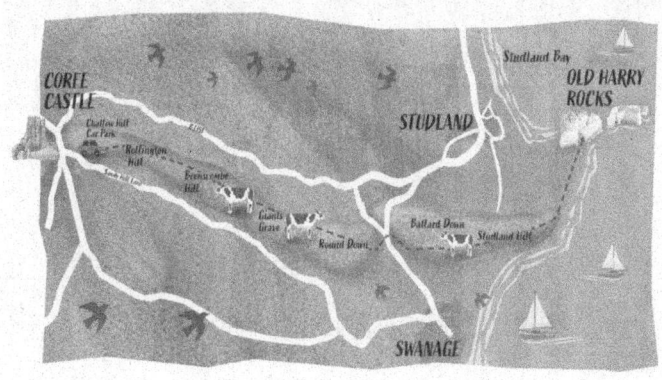

Old Harry Rocks and Ballard Down

Walking route

Challow walkers car park on Sandy Hill Lane – Rollington Hill – Brenscombe Hill – Giant's Grave – Round Down – Studland Hill – Ballard Down – Old Harry Rocks – Studland

3

BROWNSEA ISLAND
BIRDS, BIRDS AND... JOHN LEWIS!

Lesley looked at the church. It was imposing, much bigger than you'd expect on a small island like Brownsea. She wondered how it had come to be built. Surely the place hadn't had much of a population at any time in its history?

They took a left turn and walked across the

grass. Lesley heard a shriek and stopped walking. Johnny stumbled into her and groaned.

"Sorry, Johnny," she said. "What was that?"

Ed smiled at her. "Our resident peacock. Noisy bugger."

The Island Murders, Chapter 6

During a recent author talk at a Bournemouth bookshop, I was asked which book location I'd enjoyed researching the most.

The answer wasn't difficult. The day I spent exploring the locations for *The Island Murders* on Brownsea Island was one of the most wonderful days of research I've ever undertaken.

It was May 2021 (a lot of my research was done around that time) and the island had only recently opened up again after the lockdowns of 2020. The number of people allowed on the island at any one time was limited – not because the island doesn't have enough space (it has plenty), but to allow for social distancing on the boat from Poole Quay.

I booked in advance, headed to Poole Quay and made my way across to the island with only nine other passengers. Once at Brownsea Island, it felt like I'd landed in another world.

One of the things I love about Purbeck is the sense of leaving the 'real' world behind when you take the chain ferry across the mouth of Poole Harbour, from Sandbanks (civilisation) to Shell Bay (wilderness). Well, this was that same feeling, magnified.

I got off the boat, passed through the obligatory visitor centre and made for the bird sanctuary at the eastern side of the island. The route took me past Brownsea Island's church, an imposing building whose scale surprised me. Given that the island has such a tiny population, I couldn't quite believe how large and well maintained it was. But a service is held at the church every Sunday, and people take the boat across from Poole to attend. There's something comforting about that, even to someone who only goes to church for weddings and funerals.

Outside the church I found Brownsea's noisiest resident – the lone peacock. And jeez, is he noisy. You can hear him shrieking from halfway across the island. When the place is full, I imagine he keeps himself to himself, but on that quiet day in 2021, he wanted everyone to know he was there.

I passed the church and continued walking along the boardwalks running through the reeds on the east of the island. Here I stopped. Without the noise of my footsteps or any other human beings, the only sound was a cacophony of birdsong. The birds had spent the last year undisturbed by humans, and they were clearly enjoying it. The noise was deafening! I tried to record a video of myself talking about Brownsea Island as a book location, but against the sound of the birds, my voice is barely audible.

Once my ears had recovered, I continued to explore the island. Occasionally I came across another human being, but for the bulk of the day it felt like I was alone there, which gave me an eery appreciation for what it would feel like to be one of Brownsea's tiny population.

Brownsea Island doesn't have a permanent population – the people who live there do so because they work there. The first, and larger, group, is the National Trust staff, whose job it is to maintain the island and care for the wildlife. They live in cottages which are scattered around the island but focused mainly around the quay at its southeastern edge. I got to wondering what it must be like to live and work in such a tiny community. To never be able to get away from your boss. I'm sure people choose to live on Brownsea Island because they love the place. But what if things go wrong?

And that, of course, is where the idea for the book came from. That, and the fact that there are not one, but two communities on Brownsea.

(I won't claim to be original in this. Enid Blyton's Whispering Island, found within the pages of her Famous Five books, was inspired by her frequent visits to Brownsea Island.)

As you approach the island by boat, you can't miss the castle to the left of the quay. It's clearly visible from Sandbanks and the ferry, and it's always intrigued me. And it doesn't belong to the National Trust, unlike the rest of the island.

Instead, it's the property of John Lewis. Yes, that John Lewis. The department store. It's not used for retail; it's for the exclusive use of John Lewis partners, aka staff. Being able to stay there is one of the perks of being part of the John Lewis team.

This got me thinking. The John Lewis population is transitory; holidaymakers in all but name. Alongside these tourists, there's a tiny population of hotel staff. How would they get along with the larger National Trust team? How would it feel to be corralled inside the walls of the (admittedly very luxurious) hotel while the National Trust staff have the run of the island? Would rivalries emerge?

I'm sure that in reality, things are entirely harmonious. But in *The Island Murders*, I allow my imagination to run wild. I depict rivalries between and within the two teams, secrets that have been hidden until Lesley's arrival on the island, and someone with a motive for murder…

Researching *The Island Murders* was huge fun, but writing it was, too. I got to explore the challenges of living and working in an isolated community, and I got to roam the entire island in search of locations and history.

Brownsea is full of both. There's the lone house to the north of the island, with a smaller visitors' centre and even more birds nearby. There's the old farm in the island's centre, and the ramshackle buildings where Mary Bonham-Christie, Brownsea's last private owner, lived. (Look her up, she's an enigma. And no, she wasn't related to you-know-who.) There's the scout camp on the south of the island where Robert Baden-Powell tested out his ideas for scouting in 1907. And there are beaches, forests and red squirrels.

The red squirrels don't have much of a role in the book, but the forests and beaches do. Bodies wash up on beaches, people chase each other through forests, axes are used – and not just for tree management…

How does it all come together? You'll have to read the book to find out.

Key book locations on Brownsea Island

- Brownsea Castle
- The quay
- The cottages near the quay (you can stay in these overnight)
- St Mary's Church
- The Villa
- Rough Brake
- The lagoon

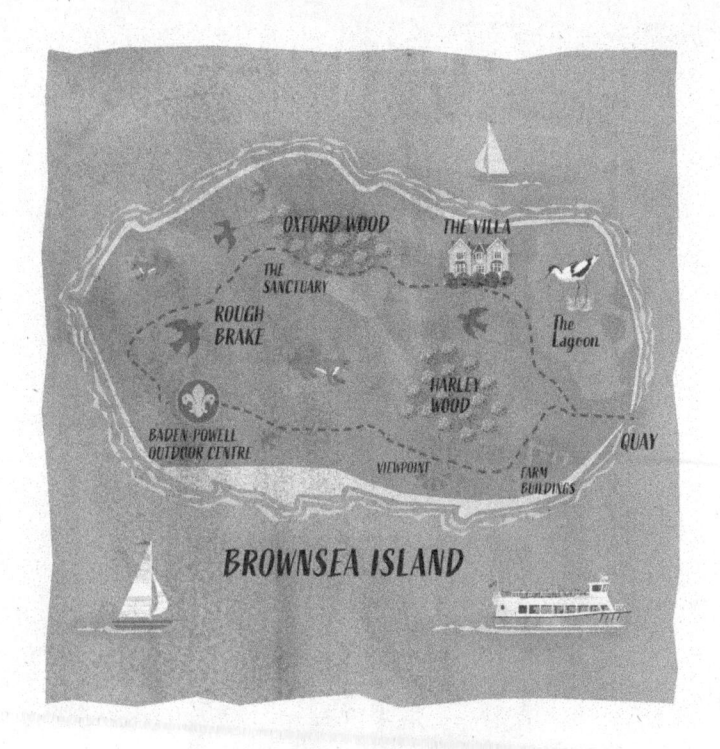

Brownsea Island

Walking route

Start at Brownsea Island Quay, turn right heading for the boardwalk, then to the Villa – Oxford Wood – The Sanctuary – Rough Brake – Baden-Powell Outdoor Centre – viewpoint south of Harley Wood – farm buildings – back to Brownsea Castle and the quay

4

DURLSTON HEAD AND SWANAGE

THE GLOBE AND THE 'PROPER' ENGLISH SEASIDE

Lesley followed Mike along a steep pathway towards the sea. Low cloud engulfed the cliffs, meaning Lesley could only just make out the water. She could hear the waves, though, and above them, voices up ahead.

Lesley continued, and the landscape ahead

opened up. There was a grassy bank and then an almost sheer drop. They rounded a bend, and finally Lesley could see what everybody had been talking about. A concrete globe, nestled into the hillside.

The Monument Murders, Chapter 6

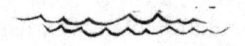

I love Swanage. I've been visiting the town since the seventies, paddling in the sea, exploring the back streets behind the main part of town, and climbing the cliffs up towards Ballard Down and Peveril Point, on either side of the town.

Surprisingly, I hardly ever visited The Globe as a child. I'm not sure why; you'd expect it to be a regular stop on the Swanage tourist trail. Maybe it's because our caravan was in Wareham, and if it wasn't sunny we'd head inland or stay indoors. Swanage was for sunny days, and the beach.

But it was something I was always aware of. You can't enter a gift shop in Swanage without seeing postcards of The Globe and Durlston Castle behind it, a title which pushes the word 'castle' about as far as it can go.

Unusually, The Globe isn't owned by the National Trust. It was originally owned, and built, by George Burt, the 'King of Swanage', between 1886 and 1887. He was a keen astronomer and built The Globe as a sort of planetarium in reverse. Instead of sitting inside it and looking up at images of the stars projected onto the ceiling, you could walk around it and look at the images etched into its surface.

If you like quirkiness, and a bit of geekiness rolled in, you'll love The Globe. It's not entirely accurate, but would have been ground-breaking at the time it was built. It's set into the hillside in a way that's annoyingly asymmetrical. Try and photograph it, and you'll never get the perfect angle. And the way it looks out to sea, it seems to think it's some kind of lighthouse or watchtower. As far as I'm aware, it never had that function.

If you like statistics, it weighs forty tons, is ten feet in diameter, and is constructed from Portland Stone (of course).

So The Globe will be lurking somewhere in the subconscious of everyone who's ever visited Swanage, even if they haven't seen it first hand. Given that, and its shape, it was an obvious spot to dump a body. So the opening chapter of *The Monument Murders* depicts a grumpy teenage boy, Shane, who's been coerced into taking the family dog out for a morning walk. Needless to say, in true dogwalker fashion, he finds the body.

The victim, and the potential suspects, live nearby in Swanage, which gave me an opportunity to write about the town I've been visiting for most of my life. There are houses on suburban streets, a disappearance near Ulwell where the town merges into the countryside, and a climactic chase at Peveril Point.

Peveril Point is one of my favourite spots in Swanage. It's an uphill walk from the crowded beaches and town centre, and always quiet even in the height of summer. When I was a teenager and wanted to get away from my family (no doubt rolling my eyes as I went), I used to take myself off for a wander towards Peveril Point, with as much of the walk as I could manage along the shoreline, clambering over rocks and into occasional caves before ascending to the cliffs at the top.

When I was writing *The Monument Murders*, I

realised that the version of Peveril Point I was writing about was quite different from the one I remembered in the eighties. It's an area where there's been a fair amount of development, with homes and holiday flats built along the seafront and higher up the hill, and I needed to be sure of the terrain before I could write the book's closing chapters. So at two days' notice, I took myself down to Swanage to explore.

Unfortunately, I didn't check the weather forecast first.

It was blowing a gale when I arrived in Swanage, and the town was deserted. I darted out of my car and grabbed my waterproof jacket and trousers from the boot. Then I trudged up the hill towards the point, trying not to worry about the way the wind was all but blowing me off the cliff. At least it added to the drama.

Half an hour later, I'd recorded a face-to-camera video in which you can't hear my voice over the wind, and I was soaked through. The rain had made its way through a hat, two waterproof jackets and a hood, my walking trousers and my waterproof trousers over them. I didn't fancy sitting in the car back to my hotel and dripping all over the seat, so I headed into town and made for Love Cake etc, where I knew I could get a cuppa and some cake.

It turned out that the whole of Swanage had the same idea. Sensible people. I shared a table with two men who'd retired to Swanage and tried to talk me into doing the same, then said my reluctant goodbyes and headed back out into the rain. They must have thought I was mad.

So that was the first murder in the book: a body spreadeagled over The Globe. But having chosen to include the word 'murders' in the titles of all the books, I was in a bind. I had to find another monument for a second, related, murder.

For a while, I was stumped. I could only think of one iconic monument in Swanage. But then I remembered somewhere I'd visited on my walk from Corfe Castle to Swanage many months earlier, when researching *The Clifftop Murders*.

The obelisk.

I have to admit I never knew the obelisk existed until I came across it on that walk. I'd intended to peel off the path at Ulwell and head into Swanage, but on the spur of the moment, I decided my legs had enough energy left in them to head up to Ballard Down. After crossing a particularly hairy section of road, where the bend meant I could barely see approaching cars, I skirted round the bottom of a hill and then up a set of steps set into it, steps that seemed to go on forever.

I had no idea where they led, but there had been a sign marked 'Obelisk' and 'Ballard Down' at the bottom, so I pressed on, stopping every now and then to catch my breath while pretending to admire the view. As I rose higher and higher, I could see Swanage laid out to the north and catch glimpses of the sea and the Purbeck Way behind me. At last, I arrived at the top, where I was confronted with an obelisk that in all my fifty years of visiting Swanage, I'd never seen before. It seems my family never fancied that walk up the steps.

I plonked myself down on the grass and pulled an apple from my rucksack, enjoying the solitude and the sound of skylarks nesting in the undergrowth. Suddenly, one of them took off, shooting into the air and singing as it went, until it was way above my head, still singing its little heart out. If I hadn't seen it take off, I would never have spotted it in the air.

I then continued along the path towards Ballard Down and Old Harry Rocks, glad that there were no more steps to climb. But I knew I had to include those steps in the book. The second crime scene is at the top of the hill, meaning Lesley and Dennis have to make the climb. And Lesley, of course, is far from happy about it. Her reaction is almost as if Dennis deliberately put the steps there to make her life harder.

Lesley looked down to see a small figure at the bottom of the path, trudging up.

Dennis. She decided to wait. Any excuse to get her breath back.

As he approached, she called to him.

"Are you sure there isn't a better way up there?"

He looked up. "This is the quickest way. Certainly the quickest with parking."

"How are you doing this and not getting out of breath?"

He shrugged. "I'm used to it."

The Monument Murders, Chapter 68

Poor Lesley! She'll get used to working in the countryside eventually.

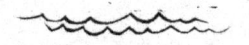

Key book locations in Swanage and around

- The Globe and Durlston Castle
- The Obelisk
- Peveril Point
- Swanage Steam Railway

DURLSTON HEAD AND SWANAGE 39

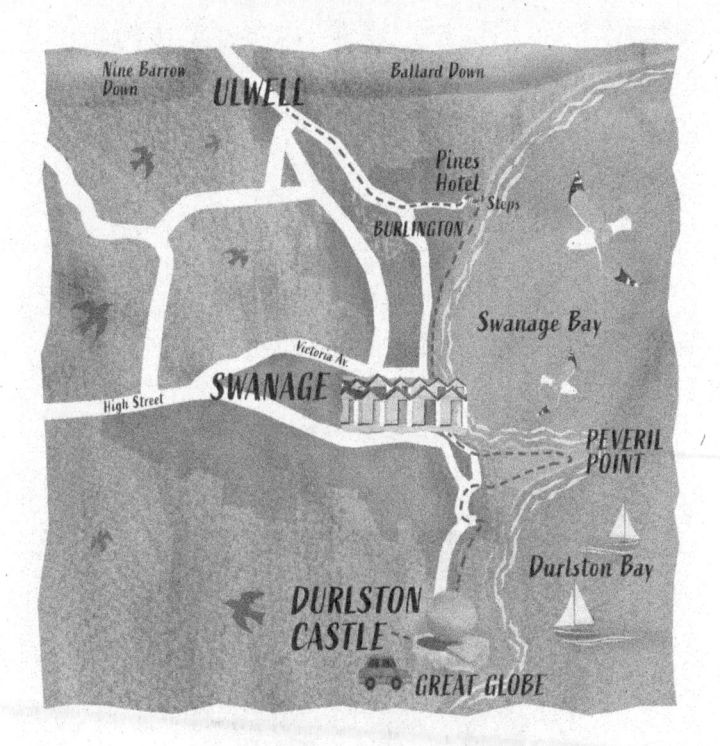

Durlston Head and Swanage

Walking route

Durlston Castle and The Globe – take the coastal path north along Durlston Bay – Peveril Point – continue into Swanage along the coastal path – walk along the beach – up the steps at the Pines Hotel – through Burlington – finish at Ulwell

5

SANDBANKS

THE GLOBE AND THE 'PROPER' ENGLISH SEASIDE

Vali closed the front door behind them and Ines paused to breathe in the smell of the house. Furniture polish mixed with perfume and the tang of the sea. Up ahead, beyond the vast open-plan living room, broad doors led out to the beach. The garden was peppered with mature trees: shade in the summer, protection in the winter, and the view always stopped her in her tracks. Ines had grown up by the beach, but in a house that was nothing like this.

The Millionaire Murders, Chapter 1

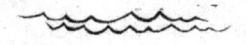

Sandbanks is a funny old place.

There's something kind of magical about it, or about its location at least. That spit of land sandwiched between the sea on one side and Poole Harbour on the other, with the really exclusive section at the end hanging out into the water like a teardrop.

It has a beautiful, relatively quiet beach, a fair amount of wildlife, trees that tower over the houses and apartment blocks. And, of course, the millionaires.

I've heard it said many times that Sandbanks is the most expensive real estate in Europe, mile for mile. I'm always sceptical – more expensive than St Tropez or Monte Carlo, really? The Square Mile or Kensington in London?

But it's far and away the most expensive place to live in Dorset. Houses here sell for upwards of four million pounds, often closer to ten million, while two-bedroom apartments cost two million pounds. The reason is that location.

If you're lucky enough to bag a place with a view of the beach at the front and the harbour at the back, I imagine you could save a tiny fraction of what the property cost you by not buying a TV – watching the water on one side or the other would give you all the entertainment you need.

It gives the place an unusual feel. In season, the beach pulls in the usual tourist crowd: people staying in Poole or Bournemouth and heading over for the relative peace and quiet – have you seen Bournemouth beach on a bank holiday weekend? And then there's the queue for the Sandbanks chain ferry, that chugs back and forth across the narrow mouth of the harbour. In summer, the queue stretches back for a couple of miles, meaning the one-way system has to have a separate lane for cars not using it. Imagine spending ten million pounds on a luxury waterside mansion, and then finding your front driveway blocked by the ferry queue for four months of the year!

I've been travelling through Sandbanks regularly all my life. As a child when we were staying in Purbeck, we would regularly get the ferry across to the 'mainland'. Now I often make a point of taking a trip in the opposite direction. If you ever get to do it out of season, I recommend pulling up at the front of the queue and waiting for the ferry to make its way back to you, turning off any music in your car and winding down the window (well, pressing the button, but you know what I mean).

All you can hear is the water. The waves churning against the beach on one side. The clang of boat sails on the other. Seagulls wheeling overhead. And in front of you, there's the green expanse of Purbeck. It's like leaving one world behind and being transported to another. Magic.

So of course I couldn't resist including Sandbanks (and the ferry I love so much) in the Dorset Crime books. In book two, *The Clifftop Murders*, Lesley and Dennis have to drive from the crime scene at Ballard Down near Studland to Poole. It's summertime, so Lesley dutifully pulls up at the back of the queue (on the Shell Bay side, where you're surrounded by heathland, dunes and wildlife). Dennis gently reminds her that she's Police. She can push in. In the end, she doesn't have to, but for someone still getting to grips with the different pace of life in Dorset, it's a truly alien experience for her.

And of course, Sandbanks is front and centre in *The Millionaire Murders*. The opening scene takes place in a vast modern house overlooking the beach, based on one I found on RightMove (a wonderful place to research potential crime scenes). Poor Ines finds the body of her employer, Susannah Ramsay, dead in her bedroom, along with an unidentified man.

Sadly I didn't get a chance to go inside the house I used for inspiration – perhaps I should have been braver and masqueraded as a potential buyer. But it was a lot of fun imagining what it would be like for Lesley and her team to stand in the bedroom of that house, staring out of the floor-to-ceiling windows at the view of the beach through the pine trees. How the other half lives!

Sandbanks also appears as a recurring location as the place where the books' resident organised crime boss, Arthur Kelvin, lives. I just had to give him a sprawling and ostentatious mansion in one of the most prestigious roads in the area, so he lives behind tall gates off Shore Road, just where the ferry queue starts to build most days. Again, there are occasions where our detectives have to weave their way around the ferry queue to gain access, particularly the seventh b book is the series, *The Blue Pool Murders*, when things go pear-shaped for Arthur and his family.

I wrote a fair few scenes in Arthur's office, which is, of course, the best-appointed room in the house. Dennis visits on a number of occasions, sometimes officially, sometimes not, and gets to enjoy (or maybe not) the view Arthur has of the harbour from his window.

Researching all this, while not involving actually visiting any of the houses, was nonetheless fascinating. I took a day to walk from the Sandbanks Hotel at the point where the narrow spit meets the mainland, along the harbourside and around Shore Road where the mansions nestle behind tall gates and bushy rhododendrons, past the ferry terminal and over the rocks to the beach that stretches out in front of the Haven hotel, then north-east along the beach looking for the specific spot where another suspect, Priscilla Williams, would live.

The beach is broad and sandy and perfect for a walk, especially out of season when the waves crash against the rocks near the Haven. And when you're done, you can stop for a coffee at Jazz Café just back from the beach, where Elsa has clandestine meetings with organised crime clients. Or if you're feeling flush you can treat yourself to some of the best fish on this stretch of coast at Rick Stein's. Somehow I know which one Lesley would go for.

Key book locations in Sandbanks and around

- The Sandbanks ferry (and the queue)
- Shore Road
- Jazz Café
- Boscombe Beach (five miles to the east)

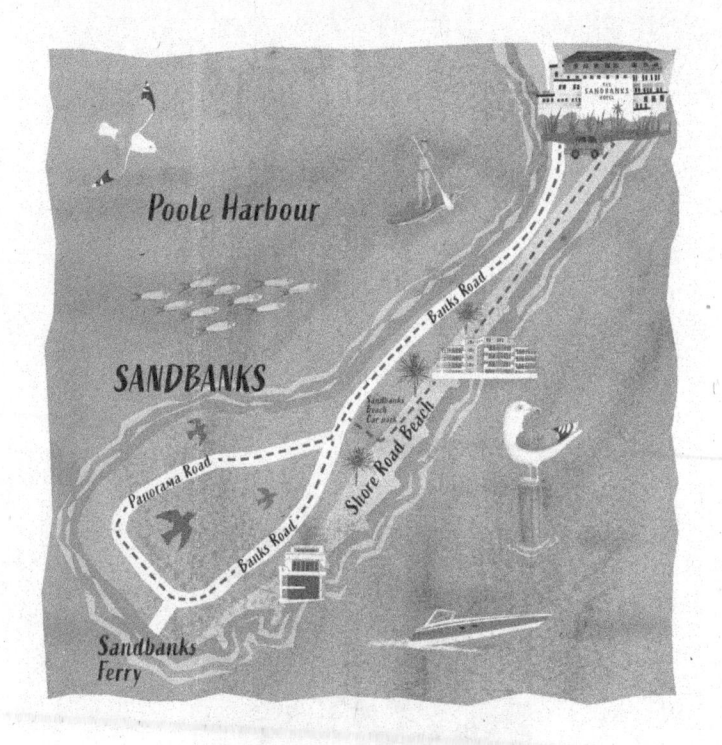

Sandbanks

Walking route

Park near the Sandbanks Hotel – walk around the peninsula taking Panorama Road then Banks Road – walk through Sandbanks Beach car park onto the beach – continue north east to Shore Road beach – turn right after the Sandbanks hotel to return to the start

6

LYME REGIS

FOSSILS, LITERATURE AND LANDSLIPS

Tina directed Lesley to a car park on the road leading into Lyme Regis. They were high above the beach, the sea stretching out below them.

"So how far are we from where you grew up?" Lesley asked as they left the car.

"Not far. Mum's in Anning Road, down there."
Tina pointed towards the town.

"Your mum still lives there?"

Tina smiled. "Moved in on her wedding night, she'll leave in a box. She loves it here."

The Fossil Beach Murders, Chapter 7

I know I keep opening these chapters by saying that I love the location I'm about to talk about, but I really, really love Lyme Regis.

It's yet another of those Dorset towns that is unique. The combination of those houses tumbling down towards the sea, the town's literary and scientific history, and the fact that despite being hugely popular with tourists, it has a very strong local community and never feels quiet out of season, make it a very special place indeed.

It's a place that many of us become vaguely aware of long before we visit it. Whether that's by reading Jane Austen's *Persuasion* at school, watching Meryl Streep in *The French Lieutenant's Woman*, or visiting London's Natural History Museum and learning about Mary Anning, it has tentacles that reach out far beyond the small space that the town itself takes up.

Lyme Regis itself isn't big. It's got a permanent population of 3,500 (which can reach 20,000 in the summer) and it's smaller than it feels, because it connects directly to the village of Uplyme, which is in Devon. Go for a walk along the Lyme valley and you'll find yourself crossing into another county without even realising.

But it's a place that many people have a soft spot for. It's hugely popular with tourists, meaning that when I mention it to fellow Brummies, they've normally been there, and also meaning that in summer it's nowhere near as pleasant as it is out of season. It's infamous for its seagulls: I recently bought a breakfast bagel at the Kiosk on the beach and was given a brolly to protect myself from their dive-bombing. And of course if you're into palaeontology and have infinite reserves of patience and an eagle eye, you can go fossil hunting.

The Lyme Regis Museum (an excellent example of one of those delightful quirky museums the British seaside excels in) has a resident fossil hunting instructor, Paddy Howe. He famously taught Kate Winslet how to hunt for fossils when she was preparing to film *Ammonite*, and he took me out with a group of family and friends one August morning to have a go ourselves. We had seven children with us, some fascinated, some bored out of their minds, and others insistent that every pebble they picked up was a fossil. Sadly we didn't find anything particularly interesting, but it was fun to learn about the local geology and be warned again and again not to go near the cliffs.

There's a constant danger of landslips, with the Jurassic clay soil being prone to calving off when rain trickles through fissures in the rocks and causes them to come unstuck from the layer underneath. It's something you have to watch out for if you're walking on the beach or along the coastal path, and the path has to be closed off or diverted every now and then. Since I started walking it around twenty years ago, its route has become more wobbly, diverting inland around sections where the ground is unstable, and leading walkers more than a mile in from the cliffs in places.

I knew I had to set one of the books in Lyme Regis. For starters, it would give me an excuse to make research trips there, and it also gave Lesley another reason to be disgruntled – Lyme Regis is on the opposite side of the county from the Bournemouth flat she shares with Elsa. In fact, it's too far for her to make the journey every day while investigating the two bodies found after a landslip, so I decided they'd need to find a place to stay locally. That place ended up being the home of Tina's mum, Annie.

Having Lesley sleep in Annie's spare room gave me plenty of opportunity to explore the characters. Annie is overprotective of Tina, who finds herself feeling like a child again, and she's fascinated by Lesley. During the book, Tina has a secret she's keeping from both her mum and from her boss, and this just adds to the tension of them all being forced to live on top of each other.

So does Lesley warm to Lyme Regis, and to Annie? She develops an uneasy rapport with Annie, and is interested to learn about where Tina grew up. And as for Lyme Regis... well, it's all a bit claustrophobic for Lesley. She's still used to living in a city with a quarter of a million people, and now she finds herself in a place where the buildings feel like they're closing in on her and everyone knows everyone else's business. And as for the steps from the beach to the car park... Well, we all know how Lesley feels about steep climbs.

That tight-knit community is useful when it comes to finding witnesses in a murder investigation, but would Lesley want to live there? I think not. A shame, as it's a really lovely place.

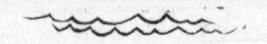

ABOVE
In the garden of 'The Pines' 1974

ABOVE
Me and my parents outside our caravan

ABOVE
Little me on Swanage beach

ABOVE
Meeting readers at Dorchester library

ABOVE
A blissful day researching Brownsea Island

ABOVE
Crime scene research on Swanage beach

ABOVE
A Dorset cream tea

ABOVE
Cows along the Purbeck Way

ABOVE
Ballard Down

ABOVE
Corfe Castle at dusk
BELOW LEFT
Me on Studland beach 1987
BELOW RIGHT
My photo of a rainbow

ABOVE
The stunning Corfe Castle

ABOVE
Cottages built from local stone

ABOVE
Down with Old Harry
BELOW
Old Harry Rocks

ABOVE
My seagull friend
LEFT
The boardwalk

ABOVE
The very noisy peacock

BELOW
Brownsea Island castle

ABOVE
Brownsea Island and the boats of Poole Harbour

ABOVE
Ice cream on Swanage beach

ABOVE
Punch & Judy on the beach

BELOW
The Globe at Durlston Country Park

ABOVE
Braving the waves on Banjo Pier

BELOW
Rickety rackety steps
RIGHT
The Obelisk
FAR RIGHT
The steps to get there!

ABOVE
Sandbanks beach-front properties

ABOVE
Windswept on Sandbanks beach

ABOVE
My happy place – the Sandbanks ferry

ABOVE
Even the sat nav knows

BELOW
The Sandbanks teardrop

ABOVE
Lyme Regis coast

BELOW
The Cobb

TOP LEFT
Scavenging seagulls
BOTTOM LEFT
Me hiding from the scavenging seagulls!
BELOW
The Cobb

ABOVE
Wareham Quay by night

BELOW
Wareham Quay in the sunshine

BELOW
Wareham institutions – The Chipperies and Nellie Crumb

BELOW
The Duke of Wellington

BELOW
Wareham church

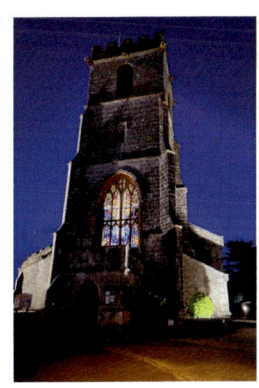

ABOVE
The atmospheric Wareham forest
BELOW
The heather at Portland Bill

ABOVE
The Blue Pool

ABOVE
The rocky shore beside Portland Bill
TOP RIGHT
Chesil Beach
MIDDLE RIGHT
Beached boats by Portland Bill lighthouse
BOTTOM RIGHT
The old lightbulb
BELOW
A chilly day at Portland Bill

ABOVE
An abandonned Tyneham house
RIGHT
The lovely Sally at Worbarrow Bay
BELOW
Tyneham village telephone box
BOTTOM
Worbarrow Bay

ABOVE
It's all work, work, work

ABOVE
Christchurch Harbour Mudeford and Hengistbury Head

ABOVE LEFT AND RIGHT
The beach hut community of Hengistbury Head and me, happy to be there

BELOW
Signed books at Waterstones, Castle Point

BELOW
The smuggler's coves at Dancing Ledge

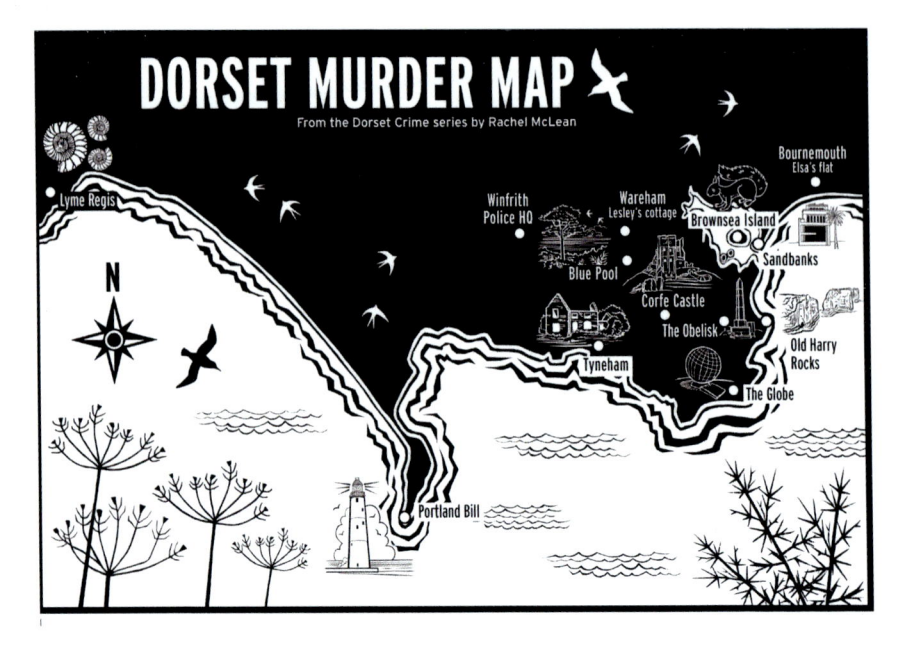

ABOVE
The Dorset Murder Map

LEFT
Durlston Head and Swanage walking route

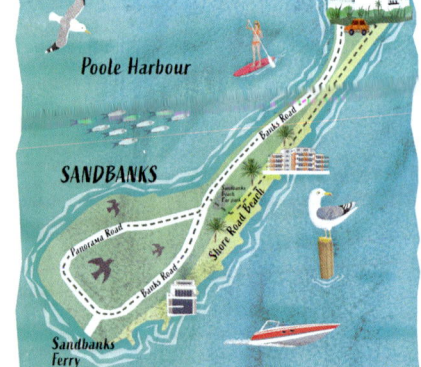

RIGHT
Sandbanks walking route

ABOVE
Old Harry Rocks and Ballard Down walking route

RIGHT
Brownsea Island walking route

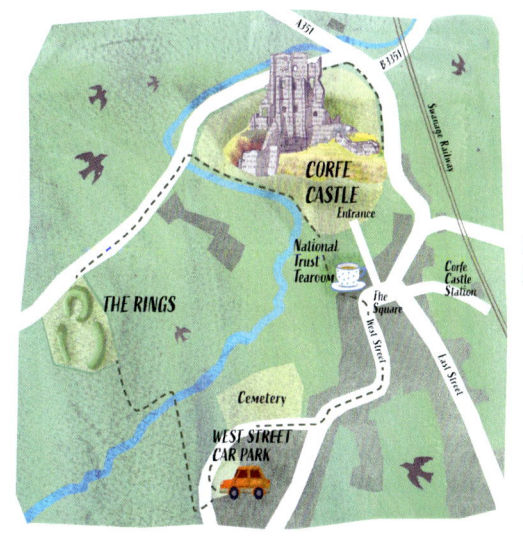

LEFT
Corfe Castle walking route

LEFT
Lyme Regis walking route

RIGHT
Wareham walking route

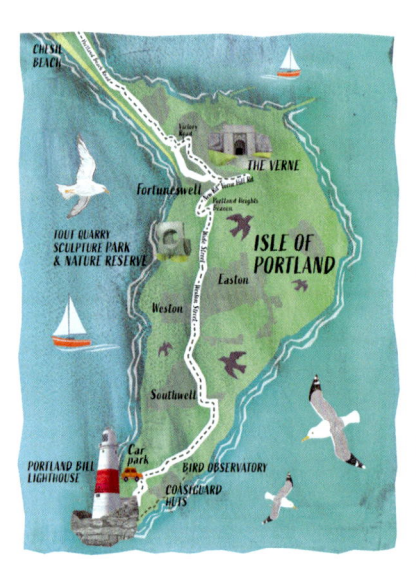

LEFT
Portland Bill route

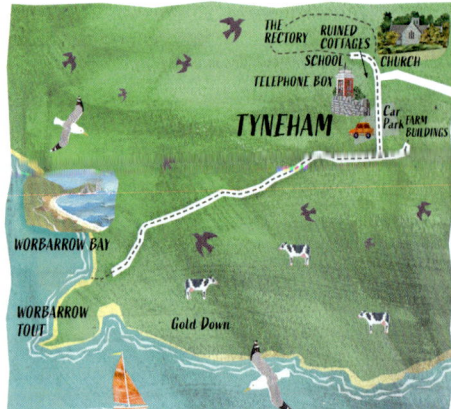

RIGHT
Tyneham and Worbarrow Bay walking route

Key book locations in Lyme Regis and around

- Lyme Regis Harbour and the Cobb
- Anning Way (where Tina grew up)
- The caravan park near the beach
- Charmouth (the next town along)
- The Spittles (the cliffs where the bodies are found)
- Hill Street and Lyme Regis police station
- Charmouth Road car park (and the steps leading to it)

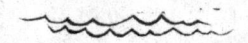

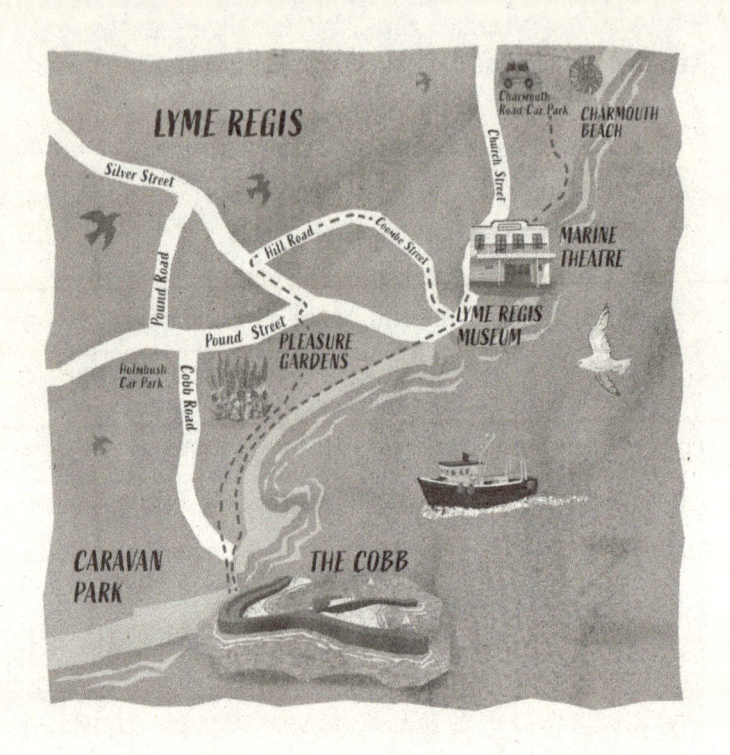

Lyme Regis

Walking route

Charmouth Road car park – down the steps to the beach – walk along the concrete flood defence path past the Marine Theatre into Lyme Regis – take Coombe Street into the town then turn left onto Hill Road – right at the T-junction onto Silver Street – left into Pound Road – straight on through Holmbush car park onto Cobb Road –

turn right and walk down through the pleasure gardens to the Cobb – take a detour onto the Cobb and a quick look at the caravan park – walk back along the front into the centre of town and Lyme Regis Museum on Churh Street

7

BLUE POOL AND WAREHAM
TRADITION AND TRANQUILLITY

Lesley pulled in a breath. "We've also got more forensics from the Blue Pool site. Tyre tracks, a boot print and a chip cone."

She waited for someone to ask what a chip cone was.

"That's a cone used for chips," she said, when no one spoke.

"We know that, boss," Stanley said. *"They do them at the Chipperies."*

"What is this, a bloody advert for the Chipperies?" she asked. *"Surely it's not the only chippy that does cones."*

The Blue Pool Murders, Chapter 43

Wareham holds a special place in my heart.

When I was nine years old, my parents bought a caravan at the Redcliffe Caravan Park, at the top of a hill a mile or so upriver from Wareham. I spent many happy weekends and summers there. Cycling the back lanes, walking the towpath into town to go grocery shopping, eating fish and chips from the Chipperies while sitting on the edge of the quay, legs dangling over the River Frome below...

And when I gave Lesley a cottage in one of Wareham's narrow streets (between the Duke of Wellington pub and St Mary's Church, see if you can work out the address), I felt I'd done the town a disservice.

Because Lesley isn't keen on Wareham. Dorset Police have allocated her a low-ceilinged cottage, a home that's rented for the six months of her secondment to the county, and at first it's supposed to be no more than a base, a place to rest her head between shifts at Dorset Police HQ not far away in Winfrith. Between work and weekend trips home to Birmingham, she doesn't expect to spend much time there.

But when things go pear-shaped in Birmingham and she realises she's going to have to make a home in Dorset, she soon starts to hate that cottage.

Let's face it: Lesley is a city girl. She's a born and bred Brummie who lives in Edgbaston, a leafy suburb closer to the city centre than leafy suburbs really have any right to be. It's bad enough that she's suffering from PTSD. It's even worse when that PTSD means she has to move 150 miles away from her friends, colleagues and daughter. But when she's forced to live in a pokey cottage along a narrow lane in a sleepy market town she's never heard of, it's fair to say she's not best pleased.

And as we all know, Lesley is very good at being grumpy.

So in the seventh book of the series, *The Blue Pool Murders*, I wanted to paint Wareham and the surrounding area in a better light.

And that isn't hard.

The book opens at the Blue Pool, a little-known and underrated beauty spot between Wareham and Corfe Castle. A young couple, seeking some time away from family, head there for a stroll... and (as they'd have expected if they'd read any of the books themselves) find a body.

I've been to the Blue Pool many, many times. It has a landscape and a natural environment that is unique in the area. And the sense of calm and otherworldliness that it exudes makes it the perfect place to dump a body.

(And this isn't just any old body...)

The Blue Pool is the site of an abandoned clay quarry, with the astonishing blue-green of the pool itself (more of a lake, really) deriving from the refraction of light through the tiny particles of clay suspended in the water.

As well as being unique visually, the woodland surrounding the pool is also rather special aurally. Most of the Purbeck landscape is covered in heathland. Purple and yellow gorse flowers, contrasting with the dark green foliage and the blue of the sea and sky beyond.

But the woodland surrounding the Blue Pool is coniferous. And the ground is covered in fallen pine needles. And I mean *covered*. In places, the ground is so thick with needles that when you walk, you bounce.

It all gives the place a rather surreal atmosphere. The tall trees block out sound from the outside world, the surface layer of needles muffles the echo of footsteps, and the fact that the whole place is located in a huge dip which originally formed the quarry only adds to the effect.

It's beautiful. If you haven't been, I recommend it.

When I decided to set this book at the beautiful Blue Pool, I thought it was time to locate parts of it in nearby Wareham. Giving Lesley the opportunity to maybe – just maybe – reconnect with the town.

There's a key scene where Tina and Mike visit The Chipperies on South Street in search of CCTV evidence and witness reports, and another in which Dennis and his new (and extremely keen) colleague Katie interview staff at the next-door Nellie Crumb tearoom.

The Chipperies and Nellie Crumb are Wareham institutions. I remember queueing up for a cone of chips at the Chipperies in the seventies, and my friend Maria (who designs the covers for my hardback books) had a weekend job at Nellie Crumb during the eighties. Even as Wareham slowly enters the 21st century, with its pubs modernised and new cafes springing up like The Salt Pig, so trendy that the likes of Billie Piper are spotted there, the Chipperies and Nellie Crumb persist...

So I couldn't resist writing about them. I only hope I was sufficiently kind to these Dorset institutions, of which I'm very fond. The Chipperies had a refurb in 2023, so hopefully it will be 'frying tonight' for many years to come!

Key book locations in Wareham and around

- Lesley's cottage, Church Street
- The Duke of Wellington, East Street
- The Chipperies, South Street
- Nellie Crumb, South Street
- Tina and Mike's house, Sandford (just north of Wareham)
- The Blue Pool, Furzebrook

BLUE POOL AND WAREHAM

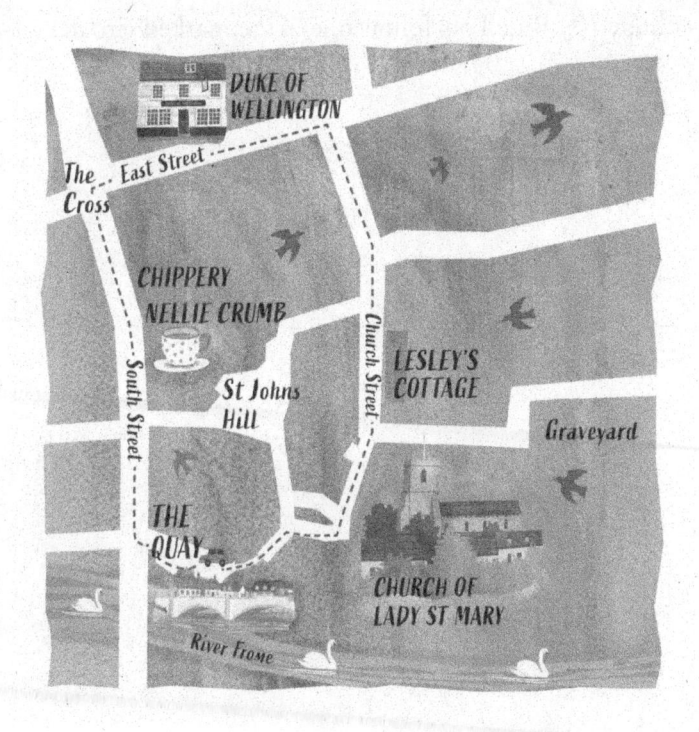

Wareham

Walking route

In Wareham start at the quay – then walk north along South Street past Nellie Crumb and the Chipperies – turn right here onto West Street past the Duke of Wellington – turn right into Church Street and walk past the cottages on the left where Lesley lives – then go past the Church of St Mary – take the alleyway which takes you back to the quay – at Blue Pool follow one of the marked circular routes

8

PORTLAND BILL
THE END OF THE WORLD

The crime scene was half an hour further away than Lesley had expected. Looking at the map before setting off, she'd had it in her head that once she passed Weymouth, she was effectively there.

But no. It took twenty minutes of climbing a

vast hill in the dark, then descending again, more slowly, towards the sea, to reach the lighthouse. It stood alone, facing out to sea like it was at the end of the world.

The Lighthouse Murders, Chapter 3

PORTLAND BILL

The Isle of Portland is a funny old place.

If you're driving there, you'll think you've arrived when you leave the causeway behind and begin the ridiculously steep climb up the hill onto the island. Glance behind, and you'll be confronted with a view of Weymouth and Chesil Beach, with the Fleet separating the two, and the rest of Dorset receding in your rear-view mirror.

But you're not there yet. If you're heading for Portland Bill and the iconic lighthouse that features in the eighth Dorset Crime book, *The Lighthouse Murders*, you've got almost an hour of driving ahead of you.

And it's a surprising hour. Because there's a lot more to the Isle of Portland than a handful of rocks and a lighthouse.

For starters, Portland is home to 13,500 people (10,000 more than Lyme Regis out of season). It's a tight-knit and somewhat isolated community, connected to the mainland by just the one road. A community that reportedly includes people who have never, not once in their entire lives, left the island. I've never met any of those people (I'd imagine they don't like Brummies) but I've been repeatedly assured that they exist.

Before writing about Portland, I'd visited just a couple of times. Once as a child, when I probably spent most of the trip in the back of my parents' car, nose in a book. And once many years later, on a family holiday to Weymouth, when we drove over to the island one evening to take photographs of the lighthouse at sunset. That time, I think my kids were as bored as I'd been all those years earlier.

So when I decided to spend a day exploring the island in the winter of 2022–23, it was with a real sense of adventure.

I set off early, approaching the Fleet from the west and pausing to admire the beauty of the sun rising over Chesil Beach. I arrived at the causeway leading to the island with very little expectation beyond my plans: to investigate the quarries, the prison and (of course) the lighthouse.

I passed the vast harbour on my left, leaving Weymouth behind, and began to climb.

The thing is, Portland is a fascinating shape, in cross-section. At its northern end it rises precipitously, affording spectacular views over Chesil Beach, and then from the top of the hill at Portland Heights, the land slopes much more gradually southwards, until it reaches its tip at Portland Bill. Basically, it's a wedge.

So I continued to climb, glancing occasionally to one side as the road switch-backed up the hill, to admire the view. It was a clear, crisp December day and the vast expanse of coastline was laid out beneath me. To the east, Weymouth, to the west, the long slender finger of Chesil Beach. At the top I took the first turnoff I could find and parked my car by the side of the road. At last, I could admire the view without risking an accident, and take some photos.

But I had no plans to dawdle. The key location in *The*

Lighthouse Murders was, of course, going to be the lighthouse. So I pressed on.

And on. And on.

The Isle of Portland was bigger than I had expected. And much more 'normal', or what normal looks like to a Brummie like me.

Instead of driving through quaint villages made of local stone, like the ones on the Isle of Purbeck, I was passing relatively modern-looking towns and villages, with the kind of architecture I'd expect to see in parts of Birmingham, not Dorset. And as far as I could see, there was little sign of the iconic Portland stone. Maybe they shipped it all to London, to make pavements.

Let me pause for an aside, and a disclaimer. I didn't drive through every settlement on Portland. I didn't pass every house. So it may well be that, hidden from my route to the lighthouse, there are hundreds of historic cottages built entirely from Portland stone. And as for the aside – well, whenever I'm in London to meet my publisher, or to research my London Cosy Mysteries series, I find it fascinating that the city's great buildings and hundreds of miles of pavement were constructed with stone from a remote peninsula 150 miles away. A peninsula populated by people who have never even left Portland, let alone visited London.

Anyway, I digress (I did warn you).

Eventually I made it to my destination, but not without some interesting finds en route (all of which made it into the book).

As I approached the lighthouse, two landmarks struck me. The first was a lone building on the approach to the lighthouse, along a track to the left-hand side, towards the sea. I later researched this building and discovered that it's a bird observatory. Needless to say, it became a key location in the scene of the second murder (i.e. not the one at the lighthouse).

The second was the array of wooden huts between the road and the cliffs, separating the observatory from the lighthouse. These fascinated me. They looked a lot like beach huts, but they were nowhere near any beach – instead they were perched on the headland on one of Dorset's most inhospitable stretches of coastline. And they weren't all looking out to sea, arranged in rows like the beach huts in Weymouth or Swanage beaches. Instead they were clustered in small groups, almost like a housing estate or a holiday park in miniature.

Needless to say, they had to find their way into the book. So after my visit to the lighthouse (of which more shortly), I wandered back along the clifftop and made sure I captured some video footage of them. And I later spoke to some locals and learned that they are in fact old coastguard's cottages, now used as beach huts – or the Portland equivalent. They belong to Portland residents and act as a base for days out, leisure time, and socialising.

(On top of one of the windiest clifftops on the southern English coast. They're hardy folks, those Portlanders.)

But now, it was finally time for the lighthouse. I got

lucky – not only was it open, but they were also doing guided tours.

Guided tours are a writer's dream. Not only do you get to see the spot where you're planning to fictitiously bump someone off, you also get insider tips and location detail from someone who really knows the place. I've learned not to tell tour guides why I'm there – it can make them nervous, and worried they might tell you something that's not fit for publication – or even that they might end up featuring in the book. Sometimes it can make them downright rude, like the tour guide at the Black Country Museum who replied to my confession that I was there for book research with, "Ooh, get you."

The tour guides at Portland Lighthouse weren't at all rude, or anxious. They were incredibly friendly and informative. They gave me plenty of background information which informed the book, even if it didn't make it directly into the text. And learning about how they worked gave me the inspiration for a suspect who volunteers for Trinity House (the organisation that runs the lighthouse) and is able to smuggle the body into the lighthouse.

You see why I don't tell tour guides what I'm doing?

My research at the lighthouse and the area around it was complete, but Portland still had plenty more to offer. Because it's a crime writer's idea of heaven. Desolate, isolated, eccentric, and varied, but only an hour's drive from Bournemouth.

My next spot was HMP The Verne, and I was looking forward to it. I think.

Portland's prison isn't your average prison. Not only does it include the modern prison buildings designed to keep people inside, but surrounding them are the original fortified walls of The Citadel, which was built in the nineteenth century to protect the harbour. And then there's the sea. It's not quite Alcatraz, but it doesn't feel far off.

I stopped for lunch at an outdoor centre near Balaclava Bay (really) and read up on the place. It has housed some well-known offenders including, infamously, Gary Glitter. During a more controversial period in 2014–17, it was used as a detention centre for refugees. Why they needed to be locked up in the British equivalent of Alcatraz, I'm not so sure.

But happily, right now it has a community café, where you can be served by inmates and eat cakes they've baked themselves. Not the dangerous ones, I imagine (inmates, not cakes).

I figured that a visit to the café would be the perfect way to experience a part of the prison first-hand, and possibly learn a little about what it's like doing time there. After all, I wanted the book to include a prison break.

So I drove to The Verne.

Oh, my word.

It's an imposing place. An intimidating place.

To approach the prison, you enter through the gateway to the original fort, which is reinforced with earthworks that must be at least twenty-metres thick. This means driving through a stone-walled tunnel with gates at either end, and a constant sense of dread that someone there might have heard about my Google search history (I'm a crime writer, it's an occupational hazard) and decide to lock me up.

They didn't, thank God.

But sadly, the café was closed. I parked my car in a deserted, pothole-ridden car park, expecting at any moment to be told to leave in no uncertain terms, and had a nose around.

All I could see was an ordinary looking café. Tables, chairs, a menu or two, glimpses of a kitchen. No hint that I was in a prison.

So I decided to be thankful that I'd at least been able to drive through the outer defences – which I used in the book – and headed on to my next destination: the quarries.

Portland is famous for its stone. The Tower of London, Buckingham Palace and St Paul's Cathedral all were built with stone shipped from this remote corner of Dorset along the south coast, around Kent and on to London via the Thames. Those Victorians didn't do things by halves.

Stone is still quarried in Portland, although not in anything like the quantity it once was. I spotted just one working quarry on my two research trips to the peninsula. So the fact that most of the quarrying has stopped means there are plenty of abandoned quarries.

The perfect place to hide a body, right?

Certainly the perfect place for a research expedition, or for a fascinating walk if you ever get to visit Portland. I spent an intriguing couple of hours exploring the old quarries. Venturing down tunnels and walkways created by quarrying, climbing over vast boulders, marvelling at the variety of plants and animals that have made the quarries their home. It's a fascinating place, which was deserted when I visited, and in its way just as interesting as a nature reserve like Arne.

So: Portland. An island (or peninsula if you're being pedantic) full of surprises. And full of exquisite locations for a crime novel. It's not a place many would think to visit, but I wholeheartedly recommend it.

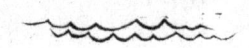

Key book locations in Corfe Castle and around

- Portland Bill
- Portland Lighthouse
- Chesil Beach
- The Portland quarries
- Portland Harbour
- The Verne prison

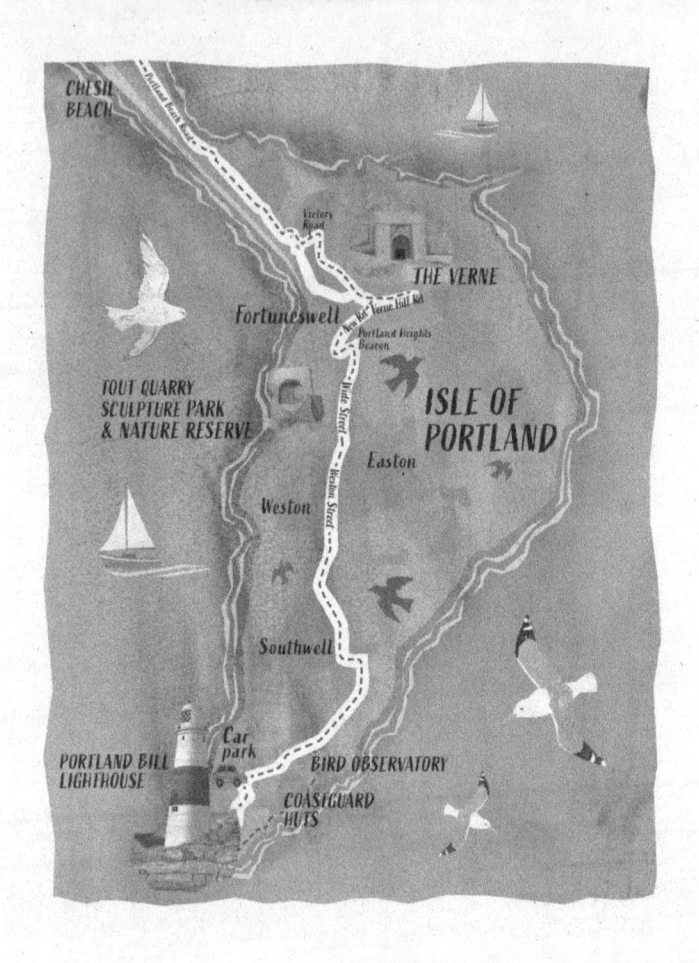

Isle of Portland

Driving route

Start at Chesil beach – drive onto the island – drive up Victory Road then turn left onto Verne Hill Road – take a detour onto The Verne – drive back along Verne Hill Road and turn left onto New Road up the hill – stop at Portland Heights beacon to take in the view – drive on to Portland Bill through Weston and Southwell – stop at the lighthouse car park and visit the lighthouse – walk along the clifftop past the old coastguard's huts to the bird observatory – drive back to Weston Road and turn left following signs to Tout Quarry Sculpture Park and Nature Reserve where you can explore the quarry – drive back down the hill towards Weymouth

9

TYNEHAM AND WORBARROW BAY
THE BEST PLACE FOR A MURDER MYSTERY

Lesley and Dennis walked past the ruined buildings, towards a church that appeared to be the only intact building in the village. They turned a corner.

"The church is still in use?" Lesley asked, thinking of Brownsea Island, barely inhabited but still holding church services every Sunday.

Dennis shook his head. "It's a museum of sorts. The main museum's in the schoolroom, but they have exhibits and photos in the church too. I'll show you if you want."

Lesley shook her head. "We've got a murder case to be getting on with."

The Ghost Village Murders, Chapter 4

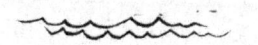

I magine the scene.

You're a crime writer, planning a series of novels set in Dorset. What is the one location you absolutely cannot overlook?

Tyneham, of course.

If you've never heard of Tyneham, let me fill you in. It's a village between Wareham and Lulworth. In 1943, it had a population of 225.

But by then, the Second World War was in full flow, and the Ministry of Defence, or MoD, decided it had a better use for the village. It's in the middle of a swathe of land that's been owned by the MoD and used for exercises since 1916, so you can see how their thinking went.

The powers that be needed somewhere with buildings, somewhere they could run exercises that involved training soldiers how to fight in an built-up environment. All in preparation for D-Day.

Nowadays, the MoD gets around this by building dummy streets and villages at its existing bases. It creates locations, a bit like film sets, that it can destroy and rebuild, without impacting on the local civilian population.

But in 1943, the MoD didn't work like that. And the British population was significantly more willing to make the kind of sacrifice that the people of Tyneham did.

(Can you imagine it now? The authorities knock on your door and tell you you've got to get out so they can fire guns at your home. Would you say yes? I doubt it.)

But fortunately for the British government, the people of Tyneham were more obedient than I am, and so they evacuated the village and were distributed around nearby towns and villages. They were promised their homes back, that after a period of time they would be able to return. The last person to leave even left a note on the church door saying as much:

Please treat the church and houses with care; we have given up our homes where many of us lived for generations to help win the war to keep men free. We shall return one day and thank you for treating the village kindly.

But they never returned.

All of which means that, in an eerily quiet spot in Dorset, not too far from the sea, you can find a completely abandoned village. Some of the buildings are intact, others are shells of their former selves. The church, interestingly, has been perfectly preserved. And the whole thing serves as a snapshot of a long-forgotten way of life, a real-life museum of Dorset's history.

And, as I may have mentioned, the perfect place to dump a body.

I always knew that Tyneham would feature in the books. As it was such a special place, I wanted it to be the location for the book which I intended to be the final instalment, *The Ghost Village Murders*. (As you probably know by now, there will be nine more books following that one, but that doesn't reduce the impact of Tyneham as the principal location for the book in which the DCI Mackie case comes to its conclusion.)

One of the wonderful things about Tyneham is that, despite it being a tourist destination, the MoD has not attempted to make money from it. It would be a bit rich I suppose, given that those houses belonged to the community. But there's no entrance fee and no barrier to entry, as long as the firing ranges aren't closed for exercises.

On weekdays for much of the year, you can't get near Tyneham. The Lulworth ranges surrounding it are closed to cars and walkers to protect the public. But in the height of summer, and every weekend throughout the year, you can just drive along the B3070 out of Lulworth, take a right turn onto a narrow lane, and find yourself in Tyneham.

There's a car park that used to have an honesty box now replaced by an app, but that's as official as it gets. And the lack of restrictions (other than people inconveniently firing guns at you on weekdays) is why I was able to visit Tyneham at a time when most visitor attractions were closed.

I took my first research trip to Tyneham in the spring of 2021. At that time, Corfe Castle was still closed due to Covid restrictions, as were all the pubs and hotels in the county. Dorset was quiet, and Tyneham quieter still.

I had the place to myself. It allowed me to imagine what the village would feel like if the police shut it down as a crime scene. If the only sign of occupation was CSI vans and squad cars.

It also meant I could have a good old poke around the abandoned buildings. Some of them are fenced off for safety, and while I wasn't foolish enough to attempt exploring those, I was able to get an uninterrupted view of them and capture some video footage with only birdsong as a backing track.

I wandered the village, lamented the fact that the church and schoolhouse (both full of exhibits) were locked, and walked the path down to Worbarrow Bay. There, I climbed up Worbarrow Trout and barely made it back down in one piece. My boots had doubled in size thanks to the clay that had stuck to them, and everything was suddenly very sticky.

Initially, I was planning to have the body spotted in one of the fenced-off houses by a small child visiting with his family. I figured that, with his eye level being lower than everyone else's, he might spot something the adults didn't.

But I changed my mind on a later research trip. In the summer of 2022, I was staying near Durdle Door, where some other key scenes in *The Ghost Village Murders* take place, and I'd arranged to meet my friend Maria at Tyneham.

There was something magical about the deserted village in the evening. The low sun brought an extra layer of tranquillity, and I couldn't help but marvel at the fact that, provided the road is open, anyone has access to Tyneham at any time of day.

I began to imagine teenagers using the village as a place to gather. A couple sneaking off to get some time alone... and then finding a body.

Once the body has been found and the village sealed off, the fun begins. And Tyneham turned out to be the perfect location for a murder mystery with more than the usual amount of intrigue.

Yes, there are forensics, and the struggle to examine a body that's been left in the middle of an abandoned building that could crumble at any moment. No, there's no CCTV (of course). But there are also lots of scenes with people sneaking about in the woods, moving evidence from one place to another, and generally using the abandoned village to conceal all kinds of dodgy goings-on.

All of which is why I loved writing about Tyneham. And why I wholeheartedly recommend a visit.

Just make sure you don't go when there's any chance of being in the line of fire.

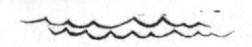

Key book locations in Tyneham and around

- Tyneham Village
- Tyneham Church and Schoolhouse (both are museums)
- Worbarrow Bay and Worbarrow Trout
- Durdle Door
- Lulworth and Lulworth Bay
- Monkey World (which features in a climactic scene of the book)

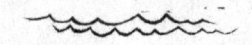

Tyneham and Worbarrow Bay

Walking route

There is no set walking route around Tyneham but make sure you visit the church and the school if they are open, then walk along the path past the old farm buildings to Worbarrow Bay and Worbarrow Trout.

THE FUTURE...

I hope this book has conveyed some of my love of Dorset, and shown you how much I've enjoyed writing my crime novels here.

When I'm on a research trip, I often have to pinch myself. Investigating the potential locations for a new book always involves a walk. That might be a wander around an abandoned village, an atmospheric hike through a forest, or a twelve-mile yomp across hills and along clifftops to reach Old Harry Rooks.

And when I'm out in the Dorset countryside, being inspired by all those stunning locations, I often stop and marvel.

It's a weekday afternoon. Most people are stuck indoors, working at a computer or behind a counter. But I'm here, on the top of a hill, admiring a breathtaking view. Imagining how I can ruin it by dumping a body in it (just a fictional body, of course).

And this is my job.

I'm incredibly lucky to be able to make a living from my words. I'm even more lucky to do it in a county I adore.

And I hope to continue for years to come.

Which is why I hope you'll join me for the next chapter of the journey.

This book chronicles my adventures researching and writing the first nine books in my Dorset Crime series. It may not have escaped your attention that they're all set on or close to the sea, and that the Isle of Purbeck features heavily.

I make no apology for that. I have a real fondness for the Isle of Purbeck, and as a Brummie I hanker for the sea.

But there are nine more books planned, in the course of which I hope to span a wider range of Dorset locations. From Hengistbury Head in the east to Lyme Regis in the west and Shaftesbury in the north, I'm looking forward to researching and writing about even more Dorset beauty spots.

Here's a selection of locations I plan to use:

- Gold Hill in Shaftesbury
- The Chained Library in Wimborne
- That beautiful bridge in Bridport (please tell me I'm not the only one who feels like I'm on the banks of the Loire when I look at it)
- Hengistbury Head and Mudeford Harbour (and I might even stray into the New Forest)

- Dancing Ledge near Worth Matravers (yes it's Purbeck, but I can't resist a parallel between the modern-day organised criminals who feature in my books and the smugglers who once used it)
- The Cerne Abbas Giant (I really don't envy my cover designer with that one)

And the list will continue...

While you're waiting for the next book, *The Poole Harbour Murders*, to come out in July of 2025, I have a novella for you. *The Lyme Regis Murder* sees DC Tina Abbott juggling work and family and introduces some of the characters from a spin-off mystery series, *The Lyme Regis Women's Swimming Club*, that I'm writing with Millie Ravensworth.

The Lyme Regis Murder is exclusive to the rachelmclean.com website and will be out in December 2024. I hope you enjoy it!

Happy reading!

Rachel

READ THE DORSET CRIME SERIES

The Corfe Castle Murders
The Clifftop Murders
The Island Murders
The Monument Murders
The Millionaire Murders
The Fossil Beach Murders
The Blue Pool Murders
The Lighthouse Murders
The Ghost Village Murders
The Poole Harbour Murders

...and more to come

Buy from book retailers or via the Rachel McLean website.

ALSO BY RACHEL MCLEAN

The DI Zoe Finch Series

Deadly Wishes

Deadly Choices

Deadly Desires

Deadly Terror

Deadly Reprisal

Deadly Fallout

Deadly Christmas

Deadly Origins, the FREE Zoe Finch prequel

The McBride & Tanner Series

Blood and Money

Death and Poetry

Power and Treachery

Secrets and History

The Cumbria Crime Series by Rachel McLean and Joel Hames

The Harbour

The Mine

The Cairn

The Barn

The Lake

...and more to come

The London Cosy Mystery Series by Rachel McLean and Millie Ravensworth – buy from book retailers or via the Rachel McLean website.

Death at Westminster

Death in the West End

Death at Tower Bridge

Death on the Thames

Death at St Paul's Cathedral

Death at Abbey Road

ACKNOWLEDGEMENTS

Acknowledgements in the back of books are a funny thing. I sometimes wonder if the only people who read them are those expecting to find their name there.

If you're expecting to find your name here, I really hope I don't disappoint you. That's why I never add them to my novels. But this book is a bit different.

So here goes.

Firstly, I want to thank you, the reader (see? I told you I wouldn't disappoint). Without you, and hundreds of thousands of people like you, I wouldn't be where I am today.

Being a full-time author is a privilege, and one that's only possible if people read the books. So, thank you. Thank you for buying and reading (or listening to) my books, for coming along to book signings and author events, for joining my book club, and (importantly) for recommending my books to your friends and family.

(There, you can stop reading now. Unless you're interested in knowing about the people who help make an author career possible.)

A number of people directly contributed to the creation and production of this book, and you wouldn't be holding it without them. Sharn Hutton sourced photographs and created the layout for the hardback and made it much more beautiful than I could have. Rebecca Collins masterfully project managed the publishing process (as always) and formatted the ebook and paperback editions. Adrian Hobart mastered the audiobook and edited out all of my heavy breathing. And Maria Burns created the gorgeous, hand-drawn maps in each chapter.

I also need to thank the rest of my fabulous team at Ackroyd Publishing. Jayne O'Keeffe collated the files and metadata for this book (and all the others) and ensures that the books are actually published. Catherine Matthews runs my website, online store and book club and is the person who will help you if you have problems downloading a book. Alex Spears masterminds my advertising and use of data and helps me understand how best to

reach readers. Simon Fairbanks does the thing I'm far too scared to do – cold-calling bookshops and persuading them to find shelf space for my books. And Jamie McCollin has created a story bible that I and my co-authors can use to help us write new books.

My co-authors Heide Goody and Iain Grant have been sources of invaluable support, feedback and advice, and convinced me to start independent publishing. My co-author and editor Joel Hames helps make the books coherent, with an attention to detail and eye for quality I couldn't be without. And Keshini Naidoo and her colleagues at Hera put their faith in my books and have enabled me to find new readers in print.

And last but most definitely not least, the lovely Sally. For joining me on research trips, for taking up the slack when I've left half the writing of a book to the last week, and for tolerating being taken on the Sandbanks ferry at every conceivable opportunity. You are my Elsa (but with a much nicer boss).

Rachel McLean

PICTURE CREDITS

Plates

Numbers refer to the page of the plate section.
1 author's own (top left; top right; middle left; middle right; bottom left, bottom right)
2 author's own (top left; top right; middle left; middle right; bottom left; bottom right)
3 Shutterstock: Jonathan Hicks (top); Depositphotos: Jeni-Foto (middle left); Shutterstock: Andy Lyons (middle right); Shutterstock: Swen Hanschke (bottom);
4 author's own (top left; top right; middle right); Shutterstock: George Kotorman (bottom)
5 Depositphotos: Flotsom (top); author's own (middle right; middle left); Shutterstock: David Young (bottom)
6 Sutterstock: Tony Cowburn (top); author's own (bottom left; bottom centre; bottom right)

7 author's own (top; middle left; middle centre; middle right); Depositphotos: Aheiay (bottom)
8 Depositphotos: Moonlight (top); Depositphotos: Olliemt1980 (upper middle); Depositphotos: Ileana_bt (lower middle); author's own (bottom left); Depositphotos: Flotsam (bottom right)
9 author's own (top); Depositphotos: Ollouphoto (middle); author's own (bottom left; bottom middle; bottom right)
10 Shutterstock: Colin Michael Baker (top left); author own (top right); Shutterstock: Gerry White (bottom)
11 Depositphotos: Patryk_Kosmider (top); Depositphotos: Flotsom (middle top right); author's own (middle bottom right; bottom left; bottom right)
12 Shutterstock: Casper Farrell (top); author's own (middle left; middle right); Shutterstock: Allouphoto (bottom)
13 author's own (top left); Shutterstock: Skyviewuk (top right); Shutterstock: Shaun Jacobs (middle left); author's own (middle right; bottom left); Shutterstock: Adrian Baker (bottom right)
14–16 see below

Chapters

Map illustration © Maria Burns: xi, 13, 21, 29, 39, 47, 54, 63, 76, 86